101 THINGS FIRST TIME DADS SHOULD KNOW ABOUT BABY

GW00750561

Mike Muldoon

101 Things First Time Dads Should Know About Baby

And All The Crap That Comes With Them

DEDICATION

To my wife, my daughter and life's greatest teacher …. experience

And so the journey begins......

1

If your wife tells you during Baby's birth "don't look down there" and you do, she can't get upset with you; it's only natural curiosity and it's kind of incredible to see Baby come into the world (Unless you have weak stomach)

2

When Baby enters the world —
don't be surprised if your first
thought is "what's up with the
shape of its head?"

3

By having Baby you just signed up
for an incredible journey - and a
lifelong case of perpetual worry

4

After the first week at home with Baby - you will call your parents and apologize for EVERYTHING you have ever done to them

5

When changing Baby's diaper -
make sure you do not "stare down
the barrel." Work the perimeter
because unbeknownst to you,
novice baby caregiver, Baby is
sending more on the way

6

Baby doesn't move around, takes up little physical space, but you will be astounded by how incredibly messy your home becomes throughout the day

7

The challenges of the first few weeks after Baby is born will make you think "one Baby...I can live with that"

8

During the night you will be so
paranoid that Baby is not breathing
you'll wake Baby (and then pray
Baby goes back to sleep)

9

Family, friends, and strangers will tell you their advice and what you should do in regards to everything with Baby. Short of not feeding Baby, cleaning Baby and being an overall horrible human being to Baby – you can politely tell them to go f@(k themselves

10

The party no longer ends when the fat lady sings…it's when Baby screams

11

You will become the annoying
parents to all your fiends showing
every picture and video you've ever
taken of Baby

12

Be careful when visiting a friend's home. As excited as they are to see you they won't appreciate it when Baby vomits, craps, or pees all over their furniture

13

Baby will teach you why sleep deprivation is the ultimate form of torture

14

Contradictory information on handling Baby will be frustrating proving that, at times, no one knows anything about Baby

15

When Baby is ready to leave the house – EVERYONE must be ready to leave. Baby does not like to wait

16

When you finally get Baby settled
and asleep on your chest, in your
lap, do not switch positions. You
don't want to wake Baby

17

You'll lose weight. Not due to better dietary choices but because of the inability to actually eat with how busy Baby will keep you

18

Baby will make you quite
comfortable smelling like spit up

19

When bottle feeding Baby - the milk will end just before Baby falls asleep - therefore waking Baby when Baby realizes there is no more milk and you're back to square one trying to put Baby back down to sleep again

20

If Baby is a daughter - the one job you wish you didn't have to face is cleaning your Baby's vagina after a diaper change

21

Baby will make "sleeping in" sound like a myth perpetuated by your childless friends

22

Baby epitomizes the "shit happens" attitude. Baby does it with a smile and waits for you take care of it

23

You wouldn't urinate on your own hand; pick up your own feces. Yet, you will have no problem jamming your hand or nose into Baby's diaper to see if it needs changing

24

Absence makes the heart grow
fonder. With breast feeding moms -
boobs are anything but absent;
Baby makes sure they no longer do
it for you

25

After watching Baby work its way around your wife's nipple you will wonder how you will ever be able to compete and give them (nipples) that much attention

26

Baby proves God didn't bless
people who had twins, he hates
them

27

You become a piece of furniture to
be laid on and spilled upon by Baby

28

No more smooth sailing. Bumpy roads help Baby sleep. Use them

29

The person who gives you a nasty look when Baby is crying and there's nothing you can do about it is known as an ass

30

Prior to having Baby - the thought of using a condom was appalling – eventually you will buy in bulk

31

Baby looks like a drunken sailor
after it's fed

32

You'll swear those first few weeks that Baby is smiling at you. Baby is not. Baby is either farting or falling asleep

33

You can't imagine how anyone can hurt Baby intentionally. So small. So fragile. So Precious

34

Baby is special and you will secretly hope Baby is more special than other babies

35

You realize how handy it is that you always have wipes nearby and not just for Baby, but for your own spills

36

The first time Baby rolls over it startles not only you…but Baby

37

You wonder how anyone could ever raise Baby alone (especially if they did it alone with twin babies)

38

Eventually Baby will let you begin
to celebrate little achievements
throughout the day like finding time
to brush your teeth

39

When sitting for a feeding - it is like
going on vacation with Baby and
you better hope you have
everything because you will be gone
for a while. Bottle, Burp Cloth,
Remote Control, Cell phone (to
call in back up if required) and
your own drink

40

The song "Express Yourself" takes on a literal meaning when your wife pumps milk from her breast all day long for Baby

41

Baby disproves that you "don't cry over spilt milk" when your wife spent over an hour expressing it. If you're the one that spilled it....run!

42

Good luck getting anywhere on time with Baby. You have to give yourself an hour window....each side of the hour you wish to be there. If anyone gets upset with you being late (or early) know that they are also known as... an ass

43

Baby forces you to have no
sympathy for people who do not
(nor ever did) have Baby and claim
they are tired

44

Baby observes everything. Like an alien sent here to observe and report back to the mother ship

45

Always button up Baby's onesie
from top to bottom. It saves time
having to redo it when you miss a
button going the other way

46

The first time Baby giggles is amazing

47

If you are the one who works
fulltime and handles everything else
— you still don't get away with
saying to your wife "you only have
one job which is to watch the
Baby"

48

You'll take pride in being the person who can calm Baby down when others make Baby cry. You celebrate that you are the Baby whisperer

49

Baby burps…impressively

50

Doing the "white boy dance" with
Baby in arms helps put them the
sleep
(Though it never got you laid)

51

As the months pass – being good at keeping Baby happy is being a master at managing an excessive case of A.D.D

52

Baby is a lot like old people. Baby pees a lot and needs others to clean up after them often

53

If Baby is a daughter - you will get sick and tired of your male friends telling you "when you have boy you have to worry about one penis - with a daughter - EVERY penis"

54

You will find guilty pleasures in watching Baby try foods for the first time especially sour foods, like apples. You'll do it twice…just for another laugh…for your enjoyment.

55

Baby falls asleep easily because Baby has only two worries which are food and someone changing their diaper. Two duties (one pun intended) they quickly realize you'll handle

56

Baby teaches you… patience

57

The songs attached to Baby's toys, swing, bassinet or anything else you felt compelled to buy or received for Baby will drive you mad over time

58

You'll never see anything else like Baby that can crap itself more innocently and beautifully with such concentration

59

You think you have plenty of space
in Baby's room - that is - until the
Teddy Bear brigade arrives with
every gift you open

60

Your wife will want to buy Baby an expensive outfit and your first thought will be "but Baby is only going to where it once…maybe twice!"

61

While in the car - when Baby
screams – you will secretly wish
Baby came with a mute button

62

Pay attention. At some point mom
is bound to slip in to the
conversation what percentile Baby
is listed in

63

Baby conveys all emotions through their sounds. Shock, awe, fear and excitement

64

Baby will try to breast feed on you.
It's weird and uncomfortable

65

The first time you see Baby get
startled it's magical

66

You find it funny when Baby farts
in their sleep

67

You'll be tempted to blame it on
Baby…. when you fart

68

You will love the confusion on Baby's face when they awake from a nap; realizing where they may have fallen asleep isn't where they are waking up now

69

If Baby is a son - you worry about raising them through their teen years, keeping them out of trouble and perhaps jail. If Baby is a daughter - you realize you worrying for the rest of your life

70

For the first few weeks you're a Germaphobe. You will steam clean everything that belongs to Baby. Eventually warm water under the sink will suffice

71

Baby chews…on everything

72

If Baby is a daughter - you secretly pray she doesn't grow up and pledge the sisterhood of "makes bad decisions when drunk"

73

With Baby – there will be pictures.
Never. Ending. Pictures

74

You are delegated to chauffeur for the first few weeks as your wife will keep company with Baby in the backseat

75

If you have a weak stomach avoid changing Baby's diaper genie. Pretty sure that inside that bag is where the Ebola virus started

76

When Baby FINALLY begins to smile at you - it melts your heart

77

You will realize you're getting comfortable being a parent when Baby begins to sit up and fall and you don't rush right over to see if Baby is okay

78

When Baby is a newborn – mittens
are a must so Baby doesn't scratch
their face. They are also the bane of
your existence because like socks
you'll never have a matching pair
and always be missing one

79

YOU are on BABY'S schedule.
Though YOU might put BABY on
a schedule - it's a schedule YOU
have to follow – therefore putting
YOU on BABY'S schedule

80

While carrying Baby - you're bound to come close to smacking Baby's head in a doorway. Accidents happen. TRY to avoid them

81

Coffee may have been your friend.
Baby makes it your BEST friend

82

When Baby is in pain you will do
anything to take that pain away

83

Growing up you're told never to pick your nose but apparently picking Baby's is fine

84

Just when Baby gets into a routine,
and you forget all the bad stuff,
that's when you begin to think that
perhaps Baby needs a sibling

85

There is no such thing as NOT checking bags when flying with Baby

86

Due to Baby - your wife will suffer from Pregnancy Brain and it will only affect you. You were planning on watching the game with the guys and she scheduled a family portrait the same time because she "forgot" you made plans already

87

When Baby sleeps their breathing is adorable. (Actually watching Baby sleeping is too)

88

When wearing a baby Bjorn you
must be careful while urinating as
you are dangerously close to
urinating on Baby's foot

89

When your wife was pregnant she hated when strangers touched her belly — now she will really hate it when they touch Baby

90

As the months go by you may wonder selfishly about Baby such as "what exactly is my return on investment?"

91

Baby Jumpers and Baby taking a
crap while in it create one hell of
mess in Baby's diaper…up Baby's
back…across Baby's stomach… and
stuck in every available crevice due
to Baby's numerous fat rolls which
makes Baby look like a miniature
Michelin Man
(Albeit this time covered in crap)

92

Baby lives in the moment and takes in the world and surroundings fully. Baby reminds you there was a time in your own life where there was peace before all the broken dreams and numerous disappointments that occupy your mind presently

93

You fear hangovers, getting sick, or any physical injury knowing that no matter what – Baby does not care

94

If Baby is a daughter – the buttons to her new outfit (more often than not) go in the back. Be the dad that knows that

95

Putting Baby to sleep can be really tough work. Keeping Baby asleep through the night can be really hard work

96

Baby will eventually want everything you have and nothing you offer them

97

Baby's life quickly becomes predicated upon "what is it?" and "how quickly can I get it in my mouth?"

98

After familiarizing themselves with everything in their surroundings, Baby must go back and do it from an upside down perspective

99

Baby teaches you that you should never make life changing decisions while sleep deprived. Basically, no decisions for the first six months

100

If you've never multitasked, Baby
will teach you how to…fast

101

You wouldn't miss any of Baby's moments for the entire world

…..and the journey continues…..

Printed in Great Britain
by Amazon

34207165R00063